Learn about some of Australia's amazing natural wonders as you practise your Queensland Modern Cursive script.

My name is

My teacher's name is

My school is

My favourite place in Australia is

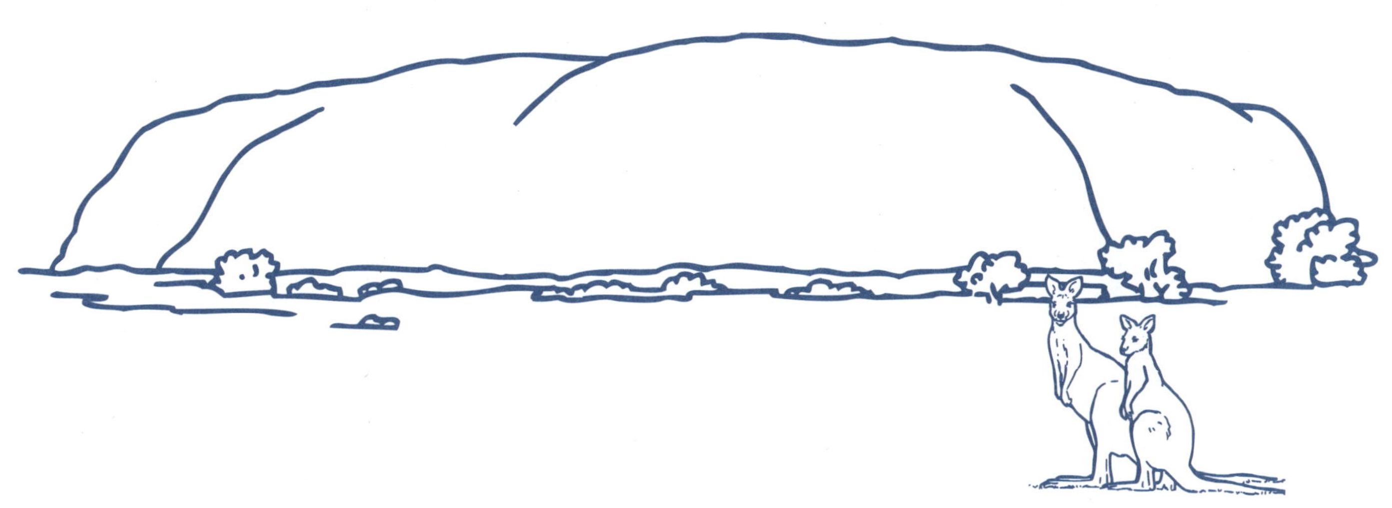

Are you ready to write?

Posture

Is your back resting against the chair?

Are your feet flat on the floor?

Paper position

left-handed

Are you holding the paper steady with your non-writing hand?

right-handed

Pencil grip

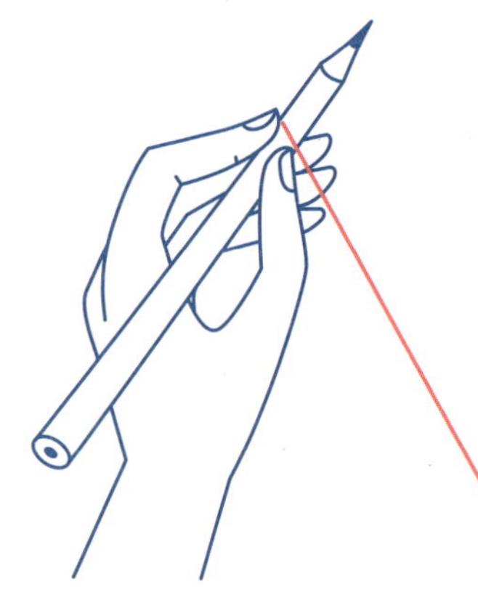

Is one finger on top of the pencil?

Left-handers, hold your pencil a little further up so you can see your handwriting!

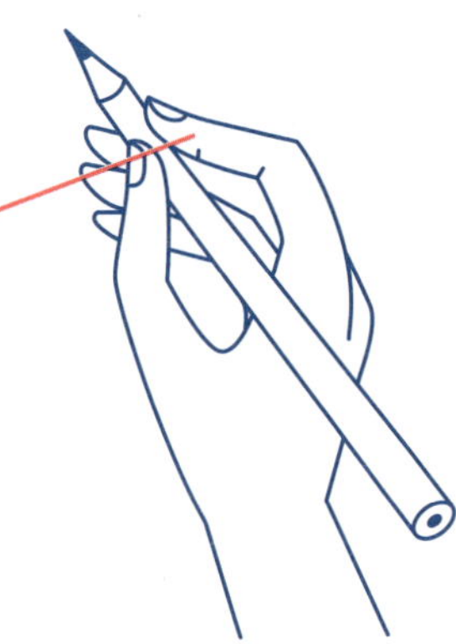

Beginner's Alphabet

Revise your lower-case letters.

a b c d e f g h i j k l m n o p q r s t

u v w x y z

Copy the straight-line letters.

Remember the stroke order for 'x'.

i t l x z

Copy the clockwise letters. Complete the lines.

m n h r k b p j

Copy the anti-clockwise letters. Complete the lines.

u v w a c d q f o e

Copy the double-rotation letters. Complete the lines.

g y s

Revise your capital letters.

A B C D E F G H I J K L M N O P

Q R S T U V W X Y Z

Write 'habitat' in capital letters, then copy the definition in print.

a specific place where

a plant or animal lives

Write 'ecosystem' in capital letters, then copy the definition in print.

a community of plants and

animals interacting with each

other in the environment

Copy and practise the word 'Queensland' in print.

Queensland

Now write it in capital letters.

QUEENSLAND

Copy and practise these Queensland place names in print, then in capital letters.

Rockhampton ROCKHAMPTON

Mt Isa MT ISA

Toowoomba TOOWOOMBA

Emerald EMERALD

Goondiwindi GOONDIWINDI

Write the name of your city or town in print, then in capital letters.

Label the states and territories of Australia on the map.
Use capital letters.

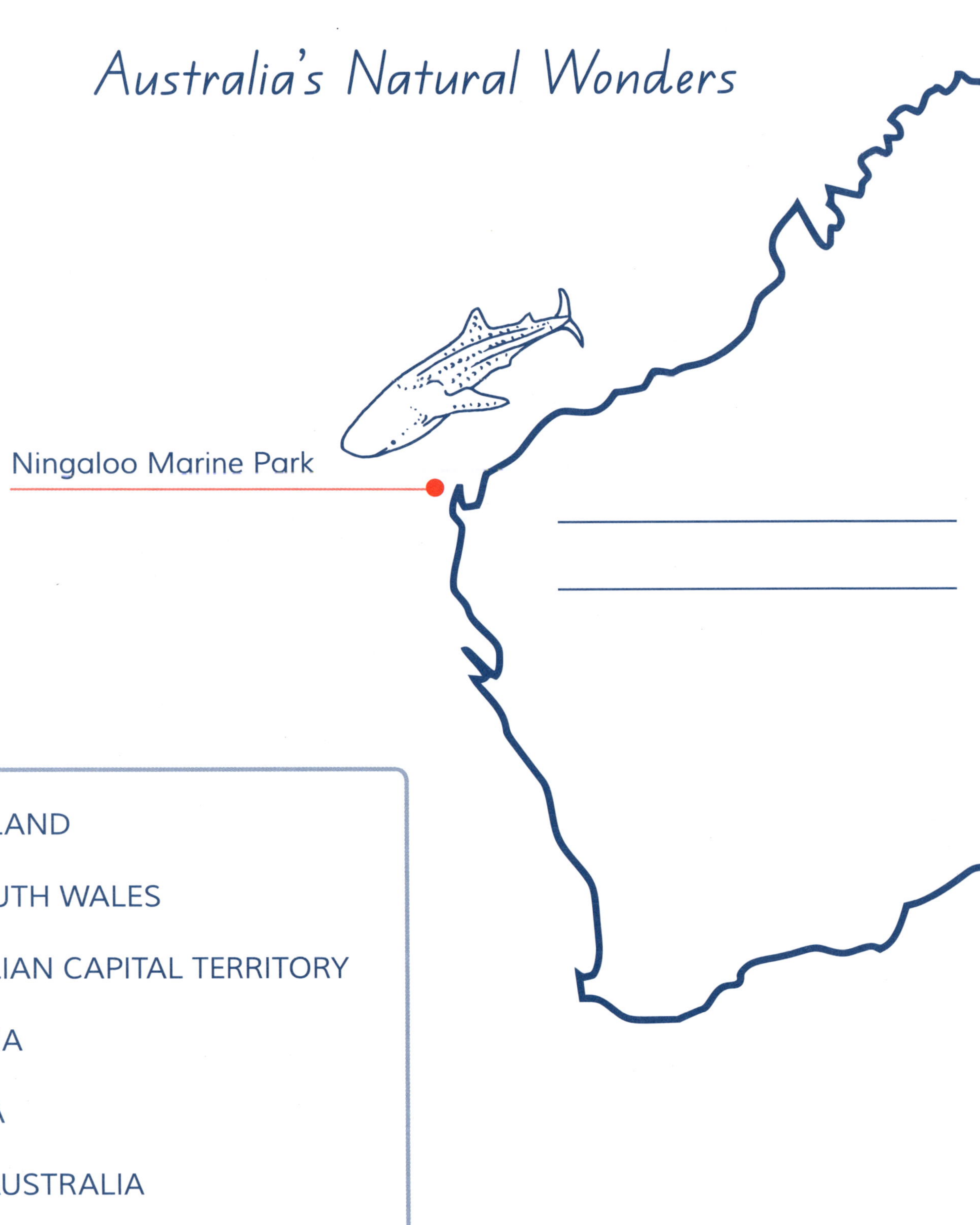

QUEENSLAND

NEW SOUTH WALES

AUSTRALIAN CAPITAL TERRITORY

TASMANIA

VICTORIA

SOUTH AUSTRALIA

WESTERN AUSTRALIA

NORTHERN TERRITORY

Great Barrier Reef
Lord Howe
Island
Uluru
Naracoorte Caves
Twelve Apostles
Tasmanian Wilderness

Numerals

Copy the numerals and number words.

1 one 2 two 3 three 4 four

5 five 6 six 7 seven

8 eight 9 nine 10 ten

Complete the number words, then copy the numerals and number words.

11 eleven 12 twelve 13 thirteen

14 ________teen 15 fifteen 16 ________teen

17 ____________teen 18 ____________teen

19 ________teen 20 twenty

Self-assessment

My use of print and capital letters:

☐ needs practice.

☐ is improving.

☐ is great!

Exits and entries

Copy these words using exits and entries.

frogs

birds

lizards

mammals

insects

snakes

Write the letters from above that only have exits. Include repeated letters.

Write the rounded-entry letters. Remember, some will also have exits.

What is the only pointed-entry letter? Write it as many times as it appears.

Did you write 24 letters? Circle yes or no.

Look at the animal words at the top of the page again.
Which letters haven't you listed? Write them.

Remember to raise the crossbar on the letter 't'.

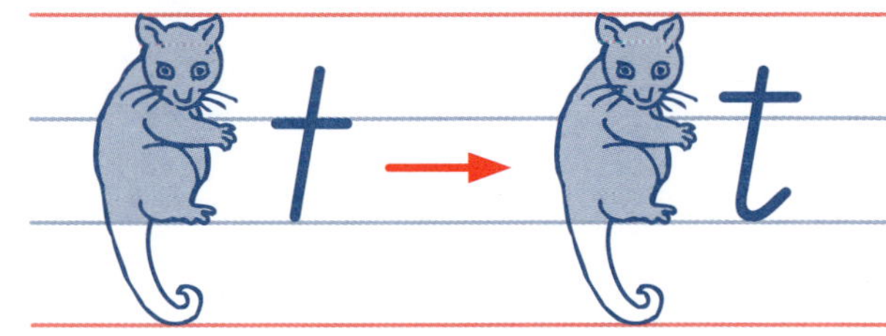

Copy these words with the letter 't'.

nocturnal cast theft beauty

Remember how 'f' changes.

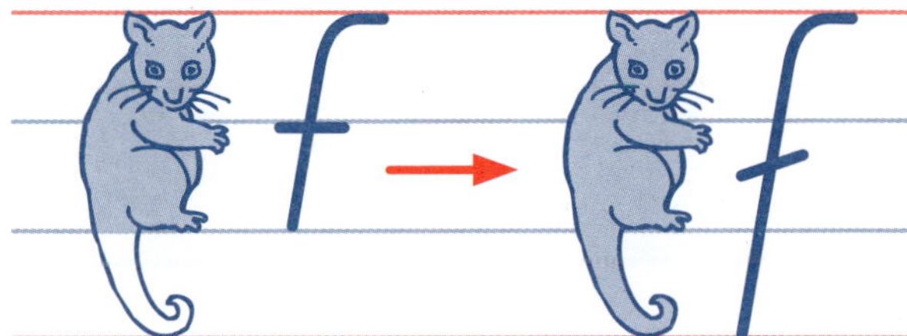

Copy these words with the letter 'f'.

frogs off friend forest fern

'z' changes too.

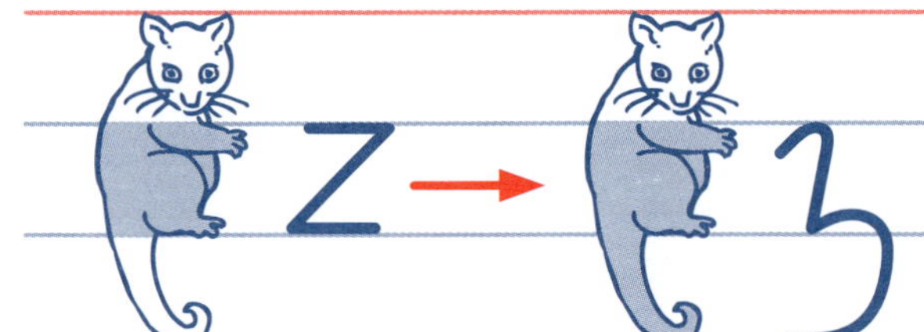

Copy these words with the letter 'z'.

zoo lizard quiz pizza zoom

Copy the alphabet, using exits and entries.

a b c d e f g h i j k l m n

o p q r s t u v w x y z

Can you place the exit and entry letters under the correct headings?

Exit-only letters (7)

Rounded-entry letters (4)

Pointed-entry letters (7)

Letters that change (3)

Letters that haven't changed from Beginner's Alphabet are b g o q s.

Self-assessment

My knowledge of exit and entry letters:

☐ could be better.

☐ isn't bad.

☐ is very good!

get.ga/PMWA50

Diagonal joins

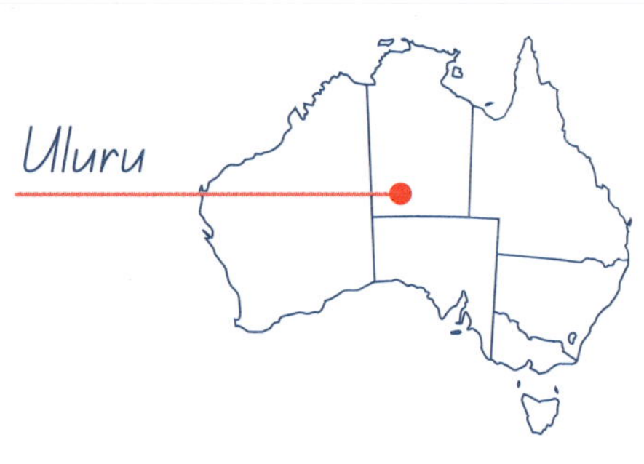

Diagonal joins should be straight and quick.

Trace the first letter and join to the second letter using a straight, quick diagonal line.

am ci eu nn hi

ke lu im te ue

an cu ei nu hu

Diagonal joins to pointed entries

Copy these letter pairs with diagonal joins to pointed entries.

ap dj ev aw ty di au av

Copy these words with diagonal joins to pointed entries.

they live never upper hide

happen evening away because

Diagonal joins to rounded entries

Copy the text, then underline all diagonal joins to rounded entries.

The original dwellers of the Uluru
area are the Anangu Aboriginal
people. Uluru is located in the
Northern Territory, approximately
280 kilometres from Alice Springs.

Make your own letter pairs with diagonal joins to rounded entries.

a i u e m n to m n r x

Diagonal joins to head and body letters

Sweep up and retrace part of the tall letter.

Copy these words with diagonal joins to head and body letters.

climb their that about culture

dwell country catch rock call

Diagonal joins to 'e' and 'o'

When joining to 'o', go all the way up to the top of 'o' and retrace slightly, moving anti-clockwise.

le → le

When joining to 'e', remember to give your 'e' a straight back.

Copy these words with diagonal joins to 'e' and 'o'.

people close fierce long colour

beneath accident home look

Practising diagonal joins

Write each diagonal join pair under the correct heading or headings.

lo et ix am ih ab in

ax tr er es ut at an

ai ev it ux co eo

get.go/PMWA51

Diagonal joins to pointed entries:

Diagonal joins to rounded entries:

Diagonal joins to 'x':

Diagonal joins to head and body letters:

Diagonal joins to 'o':

Trace and copy these diagonal join patterns.

inin ulul eoeo mwmw

Practise your diagonal joins. Copy the text.

The Anangu traditional owners
have decided to ban visitors from
climbing Uluru. The rock is a
sacred place and the climb can
also be dangerous. The Anangu
ask visitors to respect their culture.

Self-assessment

My use of diagonal joins:

☐ needs more practice.

☐ is getting there.

☐ is good.

Patterns extension

Trace and copy the patterns.

Trace and copy the name 'Uluru' in the shape below the picture.

Shoulder letters and drop-on joins

Great Barrier Reef

Shoulder letters

a c d g q

Shoulder letters start by sliding the top blue line.

Copy and practise the shoulder letters.

a c d g q

Drop-on joins

ma

When joining to shoulder letters, extend the exit of the letter before, lift your pencil and drop the shoulder letter on.

Copy these letter pairs with drop-on joins.

ac ca id ug uq ic ua ud

ag aq ma uc ad ig eq cc

Use two colours to copy these words with drop-on joins.

great sea marine algae

Copy these words with drop-on joins.

The red dots show which joins are drop-on joins.

island creatures endangered large

places bright camouflage predator

Add a dot above every drop-on join in the text below. Then copy the text.

uc

The Great Barrier Reef is one of

Australia's most famous natural

wonders. It is located off the

Queensland coast in the Coral Sea.

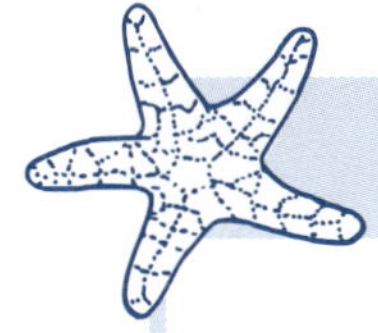

Self-assessment

My use of drop-on joins:

☐ needs practice.

☐ is getting better.

☐ is excellent!

Horizontal joins

Joins that start with the top finishers 'o', 'r', 'v' and 'w' are horizontal joins.

Remember not to dip the join too low.

Horizontal joins to rounded and pointed entries

Copy these letter pairs with horizontal joins to rounded entries.

or rm wr ox rr

wn om wm on rn

Copy these letter pairs with horizontal joins to pointed entries.

op ri vy wi ov ru vi wy

ow oy vu wp oj oi ou rp

Copy these words with horizontal joins.

enjoy frown wrong corals

bright variety protect without

Horizontal joins to head and body letters

Remember: sweep up and retrace a little.

Make your own letter pairs with horizontal joins to head and body letters.

o r v w to b h k l t

Copy these words. Underline each horizontal join to a head and body letter.

world polyps white throttle

pearl colours bottle hollow

broke nothing whistle whales

Trace and copy these horizontal join patterns.

ooo oror olol whwh

The letter 'r'

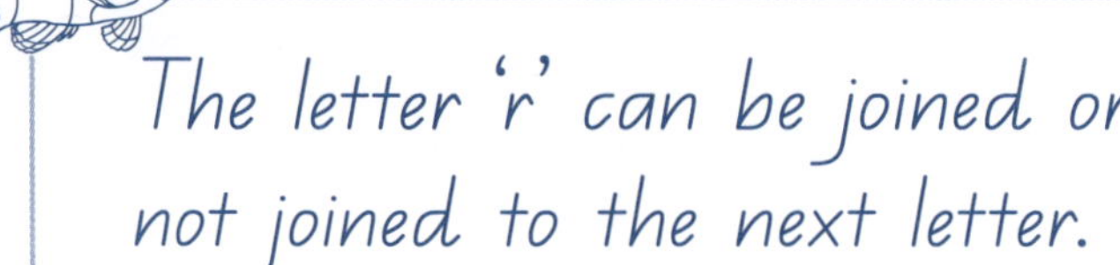

The letter 'r' can be joined or not joined to the next letter.

Copy these words with joined and unjoined 'r'. Circle the word in each pair you found easiest to write.

barrier barrier

largest largest

forms forms

protect protect

pattern pattern

travel travel

marine marine

coral coral

Practising horizontal joins

Rewrite these words in cursive. Decide whether to join 'r' or use a pencil lift.

concern stripes garlic frolic

afford sharpener extras force

upright bird core card world

Practise your horizontal joins. Copy the text.

The reef can be seen from space.

It is 3000 kilometres long.

Sunlight is needed for the reef to grow. Tropical cyclones can do severe damage to the reef.

ISBN: 9780170403900

get.ga/PMWA52

Patterns extension

Trace and copy the patterns.

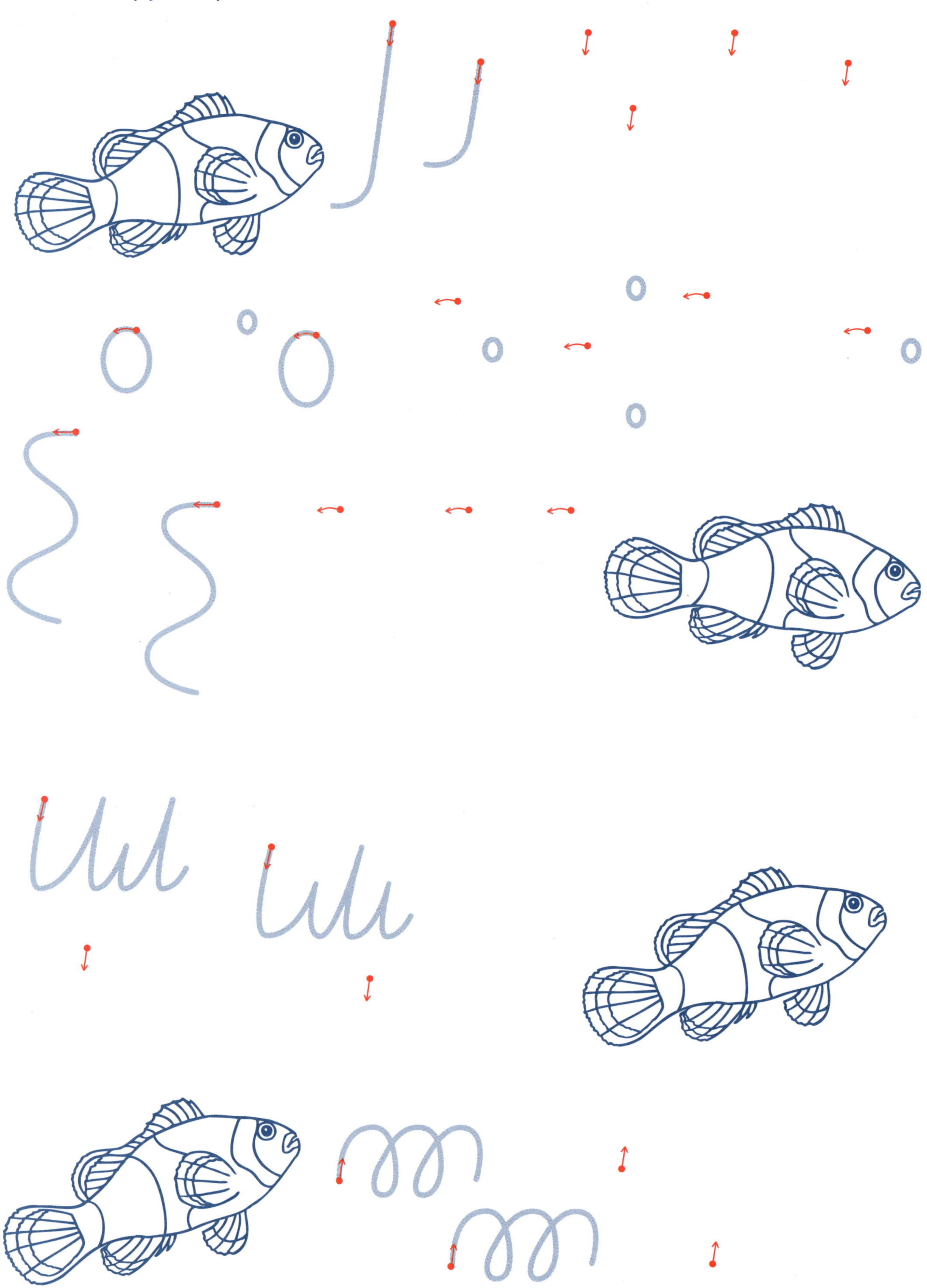

Letters that do not join

Clockwise finishers

Letters that finish in a clockwise direction do not join to the next letter.

b

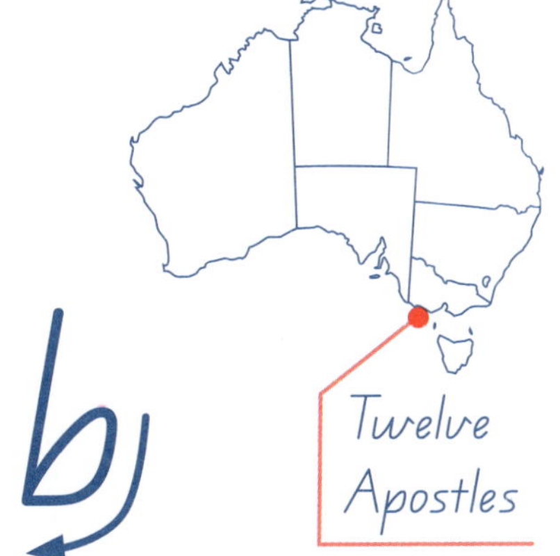

Circle the seven letters below that do not join to the next letter.

b c d z y i g s j u p

Put a red dot where there will be no join in cursive.

Prove your answers by writing the words in cursive.

Write the plural forms of the words below by adding 's'. Circle the clockwise finishers in each word. Did you remember to leave them unjoined?

stack layer stone sunset light

boardwalk plant seagull blast

ISBN: 9780170403900

The letter 'q'

qu

The letter 'q' does not join to the next letter, as the join line would be too long.

Copy these 'q' words.

quad square squid squash quiz

queen question squat quarter

The quiet quirky queen squirmed when the squid swam in her square bathtub.

Rewrite the sentence above in cursive.

Copy these 'q' words, then write them again adding '-ly'.

quick quiet quaint equal

quick

quickly

ISBN: 9780170403900

Top finishers and the letter 'e'

Top finishers o, r, v and w do not join to 'e'.

Copy the words, which show this rule.

twelve great created even wave

injure where toes went area

different poet canoe correct above

answer allowed between active

Put a red dot where you will lift your pencil, then prove your answers by writing the words in cursive.

get.ga/PMWA53

there shoes every incorrect alive

reads wedding never adventure

vents sweat wreck discover

ISBN: 9780170403900

Review your pencil lifts.

qu

re

clockwise finishers | **the letter 'q'** | **top finishers not joining to 'e'**

Underline the words containing these pencil lifts. Then copy the text.

The Twelve Apostles are located in
the Port Campbell National Park
along the Great Ocean Road.
The unique limestone stacks were
created by the erosion
of the mainland cliffs.

Self-assessment

My use of pencil lifts:

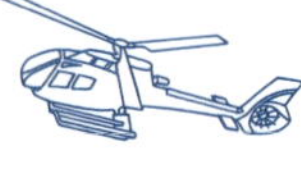

☐ is just getting started.

☐ is taking off.

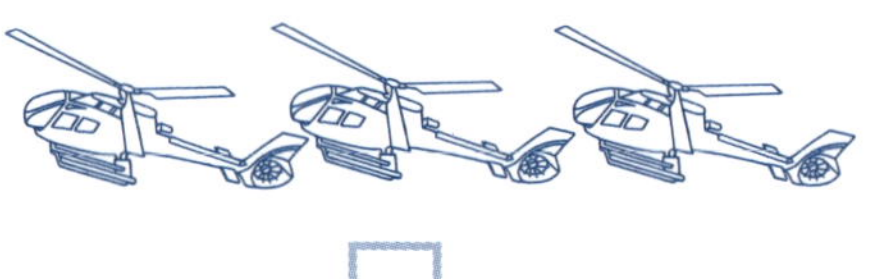

☐ is flying high!

ISBN: 9780170403900

The letter 'f'

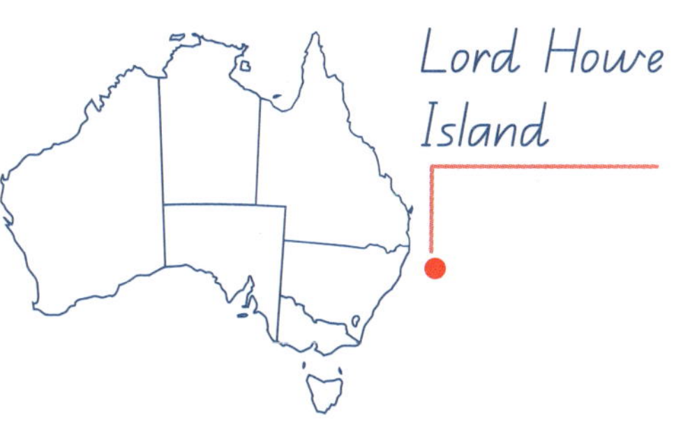

The letter 'f' can be open or looped depending on the letter that follows it. Copy these words with the letter 'f'.

beginning 'f' or no join to 'f'

fern kingfish playful

far for flight crayfish

joins to 'f'

reef clownfish garfish of

different suffer off offend

Write the words in the box in cursive, sorting them into the correct column.

fish clownfish reef off free of from

Open 'f'	Looped 'f'

ISBN: 9780170403900

The letter 's'

si as os ess oss

double 's' twins

The letter 's' can be a print 's' or a modified 's' depending on the letter that follows it. Copy these words.

beginning 's' or no join to 's'	sport special shield springs
diagonal joins to 's'	island plants east insect is
horizontal joins to 's'	nose most grows bars ghost
double modified 's'	grass cloudless dessert less
double print 's'	loss across floss fossil toss

Write the words in the box in cursive, sorting them into the correct column.

cosy crisp mast almost sand frost

Beginning 's' or no join to 's'	Diagonal join to 's'	Horizontal join to 's'

Practise the letter 's'. Copy the text.

Lord Howe Island is a special

place. It belongs to an island group

located 700 kilometres north-east of

Sydney. It originated as a large

shield volcano. Over time, 90% of the

volcano has been eroded by the sea.

Sort the 's' words in the text above.

modified 's'

print 's'

Self-assessment

My use of the letter 's':

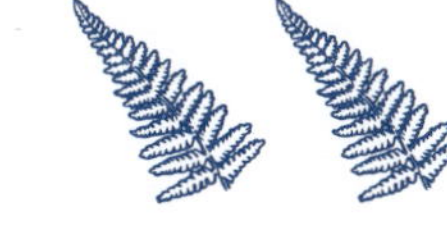

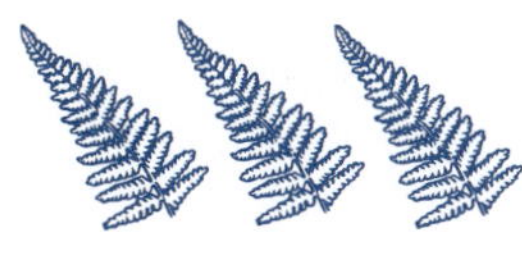

☐ needs some help.

☐ is getting there.

☐ is fantastic!

ISBN: 9780170403900

Joining to and from the letter 'x'

Extend the exit of the first stroke of 'x'.
Cross the 'x' from the top and drop on the 'e'.

Copy these words with the letter 'x'.

taxi boxer exercise mailboxes

excellent extra explore oxygen

excite fixes mixed except

Add a suffix from the box to build new words.

–es –er –ed –ing

wax

box

fix

flex

fox

mix

ISBN: 9780170403900

Crossing double 't'

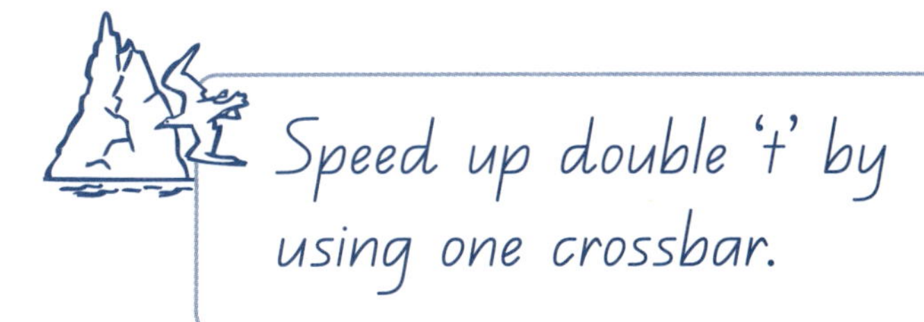

Copy these double 't' words using one crossbar.

little cottage bottle bitter

kettle cattle hitting battery

babysitter better cotton butter

attic attention attempt letter

Copy these words, then write them again adding '-ed'.
Take care with spelling.

litter

admit

knit

knot

attempt

flutter

ISBN: 9780170403900

Slope

If the slope of your handwriting is consistent, it is legible, or easy to read.

Slope lines can be drawn on the vertical parts of a letter.
Using a ruler, continue to mark the slope lines in 'megafauna'.

megafauna

Now, write the word 'Naracoorte' in cursive using the slope lines as a guide.

Copy these words, then check your slope. Draw slope lines on the vertical parts of the letters.

imprints

species

giant

Self-assessment

The slope of my handwriting:

needs practice.

is sometimes consistent.

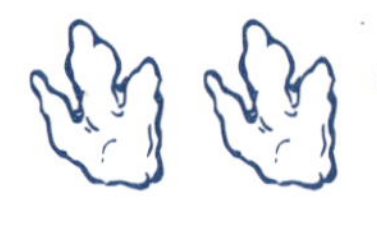
is always consistent!

Trace and finish these patterns. Try to keep a consistent slope.

ISBN: 9780170403900

Spacing

Even spacing helps to keep your handwriting legible.

Rewrite each line of text with even spacing between letters and words.

The G iantShor t-facedKang aroo

was twoto thr eemetr estall and

w eig hed mor e tha n 200 kilograms.

Ithada s ing le lar g e to e on eachfoot.

One way to check your spacing is to place the letter 'o' between words.

Copy the text, then add 'o' to check your spacing.

TheoGiantoShort-facedoKangaroooois

nowoextinct.oYouocanoseeoitsofossilised

remainsoinotheoNaracoorteoCaves.

ISBN: 9780170403900

Practise even spacing. Rewrite the text below in cursive.

The Victoria Fossil Cave is one of the Naracoorte Caves. It hides many fossils of ancient animals that roamed the area.

Copy the text, then complete the self-assessment.

In 1969, two explorers stumbled across a narrow gap in Victoria Fossil Cave. Inside was a huge chamber of fossils.

Self-assessment

The spacing in my handwriting is:

sometimes even.

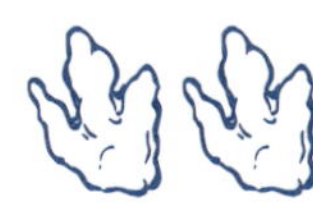

mostly even.

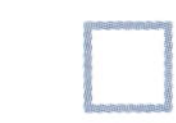

always even!

get.ga/PMWA54

ISBN: 9780170403900

Speed

As you speed up your handwriting, remember that legibility is still important.

Copy the text, writing as quickly and neatly as you can.

The Naracoorte Caves are located in

South Australia. They are one of

Australia's natural wonders.

Work with a partner. How long does it take you to write the word 'cave' neatly 30 times?

Remember, ca is a drop-on join.

cave

min sec

Copy the text, writing as quickly and neatly as you can.

The Naracoorte Caves are well

known for the many unique

fossils that are found there.

Work with a partner. How many times can you write the word 'fossils' neatly in one minute?

Record your prediction. ☐ times

fossils

How many times did you write 'fossils'? ☐ times

How many times can you write the word 'FOSSILS' in capital letters in one minute?

Record your prediction. ☐ times

FOSSILS

How many times did you write 'FOSSILS'? ☐ times

Copy the text, writing as quickly and neatly as you can.

Megafauna fossils can be seen in

the caves. These animals were huge.

Which script can you write the fastest?
Work with a partner. How many times can you write the word 'huge' in 30 seconds, for each script?

huge

huge

HUGE

Circle the script you wrote the fastest.

print cursive CAPITALS

Self-assessment

My legibility when writing at speed:

☐ could be better.

☐ is okay.

☐ is great!

Capital letters

Use capital letters to complete the crossword.

						1 T					
						A					
						2 S					
						M					
		3				A					
						N					
			4			I					
				5		A					
			6			N					
						7 W					
					8	I					
						9 L					
						10 D					
					11	E					
12						R					
						N					
						E					
	13					S					
						S					

1. You should follow this when hiking so the environment is not damaged.

2. You may see this on top of the mountain peaks.

3. This unique Australian animal may hop past you as you hike.

4. This spiky Australian animal may be seen in the wilderness.

5. & 6. If you hike near Lake St Clair, you will see Cr........ M....................

7. This hairy, short-legged marsupial is unique to Australia.

8. You should always wear comfortable .... boots in the wilderness.

9. .... St Clair is a popular place to walk in the wilderness.

10. Tasmanian .... are found in the wilds of Tasmania.

11. This can change quickly, so take warm clothing when you hike.

12. These thick forests are usually found in wet areas.

13. Take all this with you when you leave the wilderness.

ISBN: 9780170403900

Numerals

Read the facts, then copy the numerals and number words below.

- The Tasmanian Wilderness is $\frac{1}{5}$ of the area of the state.
- The Overland Track is 73 km long.
- The Dove Lake Circuit is 6 km.
- Tasmania is 240 km south of the Australian mainland.
- Tasmania is the 26th largest island in the world.
- An adult male Tasmanian devil is about 65 cm in length, and weighs up to 12 kg.

$\frac{1}{5}$ one-fifth

73 km seventy-three kilometres

6 km six kilometres

240 two hundred and forty

26th twenty-sixth

65 cm sixty-five centimetres

12 kg twelve kilograms

Converting between scripts

Complete the table.

Print	Cursive	Capital letters
Tasmania	Tasmania	TASMANIA
	park	
		PLATYPUS
mountain		
	bushwalk	
		LAKE
island		
	beauty	
		WATERFALL
weather		
	tourists	
		FLORA
fauna		
	wombat	
		SPECIES

Circle the script you find most comfortable to write.

print   cursive   CAPITALS

get.ga/PMWA55

ISBN: 9780170403900

Letter pairs

Copy the text.

The Tasmanian Wilderness is one of

the last genuine wilderness regions

in the world. Many people go hiking

in the national parks there. One of

the most photographed landmarks

is Cradle Mountain.

Find letter pairs in the text above for each join type.

diagonal joins	an
drop-on joins	na
horizontal joins	on
joins to 's'	ks
clockwise finishers	gi
joins from 'r'	rn

Pencil lifts

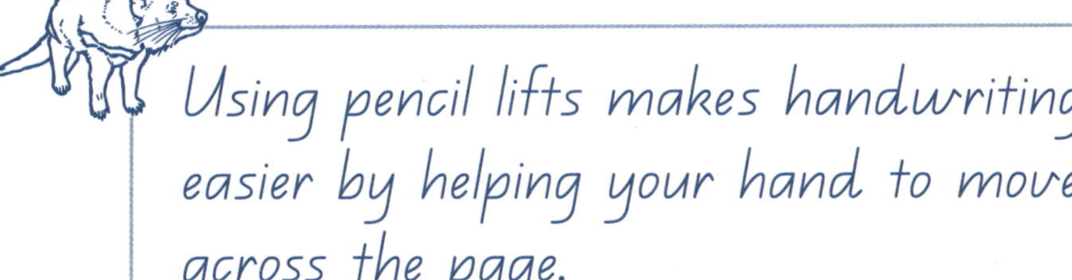

Using pencil lifts makes handwriting easier by helping your hand to move across the page.

Copy these reminders about when to lift your pencil.

1. after a capital letter

2. after a clockwise finisher
(b, g, j, p, s, y, z)

3. to join to a shoulder letter
(a, c, d, g, q)

4. after the letter 'q'

5. between a top finisher
(o, r, v, w) and the letter 'e'

Add a dot to indicate the pencil lifts in each word. Don't forget drop-on joins.

weather eucalyptus kangaroos
bushwalking snow changeable
holiday wilderness explore

Prove your answers by writing the words in two colours, changing colour every time you lift your pencil.

Make drop-on joins by forming different letter pairs.

a i u n m l e to a c d g q

Tricky joins

Copy this reminder about when to use which 's' form.

diagonal join <u>is</u> horizontal join <u>os</u>

double 's' look like twins <u>iss</u> <u>oss</u>

Copy this reminder about why clockwise finishers do not join to the next letter.

Clockwise finishers have no exit.

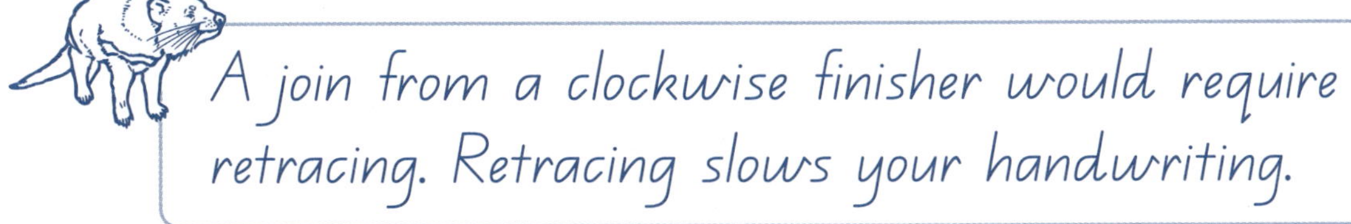

Copy this text. Then underline the 's' joins and circle the clockwise finishers.

The Huon pine, which grows on

the western coast of Tasmania, is

the world's oldest living organism.

Copy the text with drop-on joins.

The walking trails in Tasmania

cross rugged, mountainous areas.

List shoulder-letter pairs from the text above.

Copy this reminder about why top finishers (o, r, v, w) do not join to 'e'.

If you joined a top finisher to 'e', you

would have to dip the join too low.

Copy these words, then underline letter pairs showing top finishers that do not join to 'e'.

toes rent very wet tomatoes stretch

never weave canoe wolves tower

fi

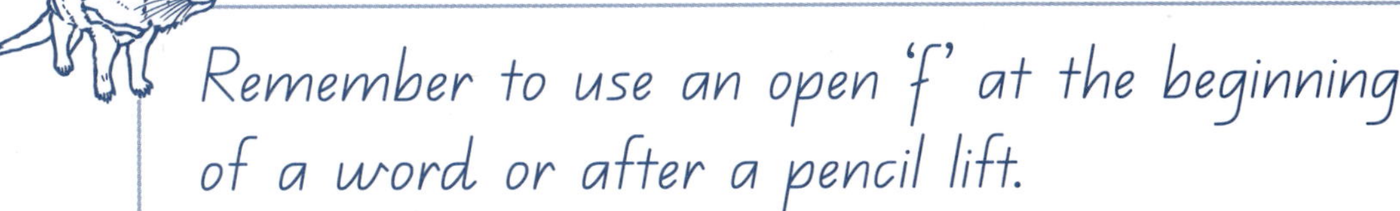
Remember to use an open 'f' at the beginning of a word or after a pencil lift.

Copy the words.

forest furry fly helpful friendly

When joining to 'f', add a loop.

of af

Copy the words.

roof surf safe lift raft loaf reef

Rounded-entry letters: m, n, r, x.

m

Copy this reminder about rounded-entry letters.

All of the rounded-entry letters,

except for 'x', are related to the

clockwise letter pattern.

Using rounded entries can help you to space your letters accurately.

Copy this reminder about rounded and pointed entries.

The handwriting of people who use a pointed entry when they should use a rounded entry is harder to read.

Trace and copy these patterns to practise rounded and pointed entries.

ana imi uru

eme umu ara

ini ama unu

Copy this reminder about deciding whether to join 'r' to the next letter.

The decision to join 'r' or not to join 'r' is a personal one. If your hand is feeling cramped, it is best to have a pencil lift between letters.

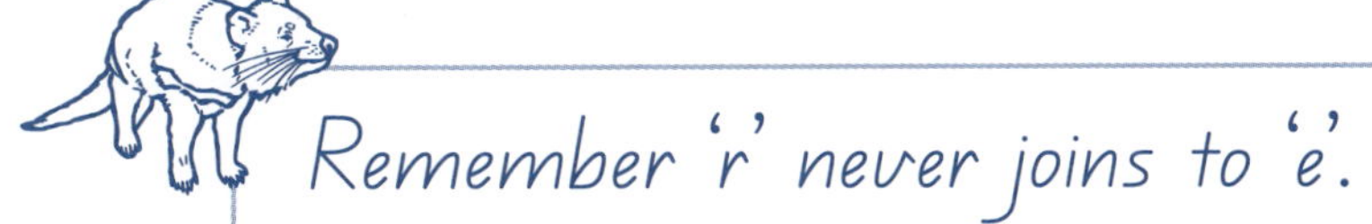

get.ga/PMWA56

Copy these words with 'r' joined and unjoined. Circle the word in each word pair that you find more comfortable to write.

bark bark drum drum

art art trim trim

form form herd herd

Legibility

Slope

Copy the text, then check your slope. Draw slope lines on the vertical parts of the letters.

Devils are black but can have white

fur on their rump or chest.

Practise writing the word 'legible' using the slope lines as a guide.

legible

Trace and copy these patterns. Try to maintain an even slope.

Spacing

Rewrite the text in the box in cursive. Then add 'o' between each word to check your spacing.

Tasmanian devils can be found in the wild in Tasmania. Devils became extinct on the mainland thousands of years ago. They are now endangered in Tasmania, too.

TasmanianodevilsO

Speed

Work with a partner. How many times can you write 'extinct' in one minute?

extinct

[ ] times

Circle your most legible word.

Practising Queensland Modern Cursive script

Practise your double-letter joins. Copy these words.

Ningaloo Marine Park

Ningaloo Reef harmless

tonnes allow feeders bubbles small

supporter stunning common

attractive swimming feeling

List the double-letter pairs from the words above.

Remember you can cross double 't' in one stroke if you wish.

Try writing the words with double 't' both ways.

bottom bottom pattern pattern

mattress mattress getting getting

Test your knowledge of joins. Copy the words, then identify join pairs in each group.

magnificent unhappy amazement

drop-on join pairs

dangerous hundred afterwards

diagonal join pairs

crouch underground strongest

horizontal join pairs

properly brilliant join straight

clockwise finishers that don't join to the next letter

colourful nowhere smoothly

top finishers joining to head and body letters

For each word below, write its base word beside it, using cursive. Take care with spelling.

increased	connection
unhealthy	smaller
diving	largest
snorkelling	safest
equipment	daily
protection	sunny

Complete the table. Show how adjectives can change to make comparisons.

big	bigger	biggest
	longer	
large		
		healthiest
cold		
	younger	
		strongest

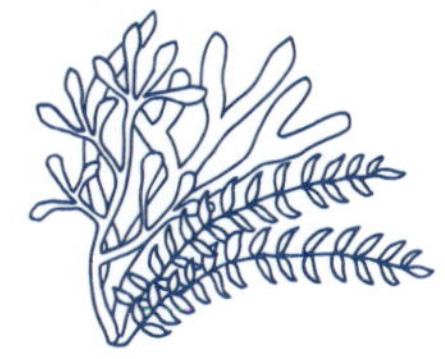

Add a word from the box to make a compound word, then write the compound word below using cursive.

side life line back site light take way
set way van flower less fire tides

rip______ coast______ camp______

camper______ high______ wild______

hump______ camp______ over______

along______ sun______ sun______

breath______ sun______ gate______

How many compound words can you make starting with 'every-' or 'some-' and ending with a word from the box?

get.ga/PMWA57

times where body one thing how day

Which suffix can you use to build new words?
Take care with spelling.

-er -ed -ing -ly

dive

add

deep

clear

breath

quick

Using cursive, add the suffix '-less' to these words.

power care end fear rest taste use harm help

Add missing words from the word bank below, then copy the whole text.

whales Shark teeth fish wide whales Whale

The Whale ________ is the largest

________ in the sea. It is as large

as many ________ but it is a fish,

not a mammal. The mouth of a

________ Shark can be up to

1.5 metres ________ and can contain

300 rows of tiny ________.

Even though it is a fish, it is a

filter feeder like many ________.

Write the sentence beginnings in the order they are numbered below, then choose the correct sentence ending. Use cursive.

1. Ningaloo Reef is located	over 240 kilometres.
2. It is one of the longest reefs	in and around the reef.
3. The reef stretches	to swim with the harmless Whale Shark.
4. Huge numbers of animals live	off the coast of Western Australia.
5. People from far away come	in the world.

Copy each word, then write a synonym, or word with a similar meaning, beside it.

under → under → beneath

vibrant →

quiet →

difficult →

later →

achievable →

risky →

sturdy →

worried →

Copy each word, then write an antonym, or word of opposite meaning, beside it.

impossible → impossible → possible

above →

brave →

weakest →

safe →

dull →

disbelieve →

before →

noisy →

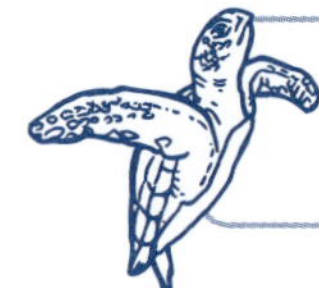

Regular handwriting practice helps to build endurance.

Rewrite the text in the box below in your best cursive handwriting.

My visit to the reef was fascinating! Just by bending over and putting my mask on the surface of the water, I had an incredible view of this marine environment. The purple and pink colours of the coral were quite striking. My sister, Isla, saw a school of clownfish. There were several of them swimming along together.

Independent writing activity

Write a short recount, using cursive, about a memorable time you spent in nature.

Remember, a recount must have:

- an orientation (where, when, who, why)
- a sequence of events
- a personal comment.

Teacher observation guide

Student is: left-handed ☐ right-handed ☐

Student demonstrates correct posture, paper position and pencil grip. ☐

Student uses writing lines with accuracy. ☐

Student forms the Beginner's Alphabet (lower-case and capital letters) with accuracy. ☐

Student can write numerals with accuracy. ☐

Student forms the exit and entry letters with accuracy, including the letters that change (f, t, z). ☐

Student forms the following joins with accuracy:

- diagonal joins ☐
- drop-on joins ☐
- horizontal joins ☐
- 'f' joins ☐
- 's' joins ☐
- 'x' joins ☐

Student can identify the letters that do not join in Modern Cursive script. ☐

Student can convert between scripts: print, cursive and capital letters. ☐

Student can copy a complete passage of text with accuracy using Modern Cursive script. ☐

Student can identify when a pencil lift is required. ☐

Student has an understanding of factors that influence legibility (slope, spacing, speed). ☐

Student can self-assess with accuracy. ☐

Student can write a self-composed text with accuracy using Modern Cursive script. ☐

Notes:

....

....

Date:

....

CERTIFICATE

get.ga/PMWC6